Dear Mr. Nice Guard Man

Love letters to the people of South Korea

Ruth M. Youn

Some names have been changed to protect the privacy of individuals.

Printed in the United States of America
Cover design by Donna Marie Hart
Book formatting by Frostbite Publishing
Photos included belong to the author's collection.

First Paperback Edition 2017

Contents

For Ji eun

Preface

Today is January 12, 2017 and I am finally wrapping up this little collection of essays, written in the form of letters. It's been nearly three years since I've touched these essays and much has changed since. I've moved from a large, urban city in South Korea, to a smallish, rural-like town in the United States. I've transitioned from being a mother of an infant to a mother of a brave and tenderhearted four-year-old, who proudly proclaims that she is "from Korea!" My husband and I used to live in a rented one-room studio; now we own a three-bedroom home. Previously, I viewed life in Korea through the lens of a foreigner—distanced by language, custom and culture. Now, I view life in the United States as a native, but as one who sees her country in the context of a larger world.

Moving across the ocean to live and work was a great risk. But the word *risk-taker* doesn't really describe my personality. *Risk-calculator* is more like it. Trying a new route home or a different entrée at a favorite restaurant can be too much to ask. What if I got lost? What if the food was terrible and I went home hungry?

When my husband proposed going to South Korea in 2009 to

seek a career change, I carefully filed away those calculations along with dishes and cookware into boxes for storage. I had never been there, never studied the language, nor had friends nor relatives to call upon arrival. But it sounded pretty adventurous. I thought to myself, sure, why not?

Initially, my new life in Seoul was characterized by a different kind of risk—one that never crossed my mind as I was ticking off the pros and cons—the risk of injury to my personal pride and sense of independence. Stepping out the door each morning was a feat requiring earnest emotional fortitude. Arriving illiterate in Korean wasn't a smart move, but I didn't have much time to remedy that dilemma. I was riding a huge learning curve as I struggled to command the attention of hundreds of fifth graders who preferred to play outside, instead of tediously repeating phrases in English. Any sign of defiance was intimidating. I felt completely inadequate as an educator in a foreign school system, separated linguistically from my students and Korean colleagues.

Aside from the occupational challenges, life outside of work was no easier. The daily tasks that I once took for granted became difficult to solve in this new context. How do I make this laundry machine work? This shirt needs new buttons—but how do I find buttons and a seamstress? And when I find the seamstress, what are the right words to describe what I need? Where can I find star anise to cook this Chinese recipe? Is there a gynecologist that can speak English? Some thoughts were more troubling: I'm not adjusting so well to life here. How do I find a therapist who can speak English?

I wanted to figure it all out myself, afraid to bother my Korean colleagues. Much to my chagrin, it was impossible to accomplish this without assistance. For a hyper-independent woman as myself, this was a major source of grief. Having already studied several languages, completed a college degree, begun a career in my home country and started investing in stocks, I had arrived feeling self-assured. Comparing my current reality in Seoul to this modest checklist of adult accomplishments left me feeling like a child, or perhaps a person with a disability — pitied, ignored, even belittled by others. Hardly able to find the words to ask for information, it was embarrassing to be misunderstood or to misunderstand others.

Days, weeks and months passed, each moment presenting new challenges, but also important learning experiences. After a bit of experimentation, I marked the laundry machine buttons "1" "2" and "3" with indelible ink, ensuring I wouldn't forget the settings in the future. I learned to read Korean letters on my own and acquired a shiny new electronic dictionary from my cousin (this was before smartphones were smart enough to have a built-in dictionary!) Thrilled to have overcome illiteracy, I would stare intensely out the bus windows during a commute, soundlessly mouthing each syllable on the signs outside. I began Korean language classes at night so I could learn to speak full sentences, after which I often explained (with a great sense of relief) to curious shopkeepers why my Korean was so broken: "I'm Taiwanese, but I am from America." To my surprise, many were quite friendly and often threw a few extra oranges into my grocery bag, or offered a complimentary dish of warm cookies to accompany my coffee. *Service*, they would say in Konglish[1], smiling. A conversation with a Korean barista my

---

[1] Konglish is a term derived from the blending of the words "Korean" and "English." Konglish refers to words that are borrowed from the English language and assigned meanings that are uniquely Korean. In some instances, Konglish can refer to a blending of Korean and English words to create an entirely new word that only makes sense in

age led to an unexpected gift of friendship. Texting each other questions about English and Korean, she and I exchanged book recommendations and encouraged each other in our endeavors to pursue writing professionally.

More than anything, the process of simply walking out the door each morning to meet a new day taught me the value of letting go of calculation and the anticipation of failure. After all, it would be a loss to spend each day focusing on the risk of failure to communicate, or the very common risk of feeling vulnerable and insecure as a foreigner. Through trial and error, and a little perseverance, I've seen the tremendous potential for personal growth. I've experienced the kindness of others as well as gained empathy for those encountering similar dilemmas. I'd say that moving to Seoul was certainly worth the risk. Acknowledging the difficulties with gratitude, I re-read these essays recently and was surprised to see something very different.

When I read them aloud to my sister, I felt uncomfortably aware of how depressed my stories seemed—a sad little rain cloud hanging over each word, occasionally punctuated by lightning flashes of frustration or anger. Afterwards, she mentioned that I used the word "satiate" multiple times.

I didn't notice this before, but yes, I had used that word on several occasions. It revealed to me a new aspect of what I was trying to express that spring of 2014, when my husband and I were preparing to move back to the United States. I saw in these essays an intense hunger that needed to be satisfied. This hunger was literal—I was so hungry for foods that would comfort and fill me, because for a time, Korean food did not. This

---

the Korean context. In this particular case, the English word *service* is used in the Korean context to mean "for free," or the colloquial "on the house."

hunger was also figurative—I was craving meaningful human connection, to feel understood, validated and purposeful in an unfamiliar society. I think there must be some relationship between hunger and sadness. Consistent hunger makes you feel empty and tired, as if you are forcing yourself to survive without the nourishing strength that comes from eating well, and believing that you are both loved well and are loving others well.

This is what this collection of stories is about. It is not that every moment of those five years was lived in a state of deprivation—no, there were very special friendships built over delicious home-cooked meals and travels in beautiful places for which I am so grateful. Instead, my writing describes the undertone of hunger humming beneath the many positive experiences. I wrote to draw meaning from it, and to honor the connections I made with the people of Korea—ones that I could not go back and speak with due to a language barrier or circumstances. I write also for my daughter—to record details about the life I led overseas, the place where she was born. By the time she is old enough to return for travel or work, it will have changed dramatically. And finally, I write for you.

Although the geographic context of the writing is most understood by the reader who has firsthand knowledge of life in Korea, I believe that the nuances shared here—both the moments of delight and sometimes disappointment—are ones we all share as people, regardless of our current country of residence. I hope that what you read gives you a better understanding of your own life experiences and that you also feel you've made a meaningful connection as a result.

Ruth M. Youn

January 2017

Seoul, South Korea, January 2014.

Acknowledgements

Some passages in this book appeared in a slightly different form in the online magazine *Seoulist*. Permission to reprint these passages is gratefully acknowledged.

Thank you Yaeri for giving me the chance to write for a public audience for the very first time so many years ago. I will forever be grateful to you, Jacqui, Meagan, and Sonja — the Seoulist Sisters — for your support as fellow creatives and dear friends.

Donna, you've been a part of the journey since the beginning — helping pack the dishes and cookware before the move to Korea. Thank you for jumping on board in the late stages of this book to contribute your illustrations and moral support.

To Paul — without you, I definitely would not have moved to Korea. I swore up and down I'd never live in Asia, but somehow you convinced me to do it anyway. You promised as long as I was with you, I'd never be bored. You were right!

Dear Mr. Nice Guard Man

Love letters to the people of South Korea

Sir, at the Bank

I used to know your name. When my husband and I first moved to Gugi-dong, you helped set up our accounts. It took nearly two hours, so in that time we all got to know each other pretty well. Your English was great because you studied abroad in Kansas. When you stopped working at the bank near the elementary school, I called the customer service center to find you. I had a special question to ask.

You see, I was new to the country — and new to the level of trust accorded between strangers. I discovered that while I was away at work, our landlord had come into our home. I guess it made sense that she had the key, but it made me uneasy to think that she would enter while we were gone.

How did I know she had come in? Easy. I left for work with the sink completely full of dirty dishes and no dish soap (we'd run out the day before). When I came home, the sink was empty, sparkling clean, and there was a new bottle of Sugar Bubble perched on the countertop. A few weeks later, I was sick in bed while my husband was teaching. I was trying to sleep off the flu when I heard a repairman let himself into our house. I freaked out. If I hadn't been home, I wouldn't have known that any-one—let alone a complete stranger—had come in. Not thinking we needed to be notified ahead of time, the landlord had called him to check on the condition of the roof and handed him the key.

After that, I started to worry about the security of our pass-ports and the several hundred US dollars we had hidden as emergency money. In the United States, we keep our valuables at the bank. For a monthly fee, important items such as docu-ments or heirloom jewelry can be stored in the vault. So I thought, there must be something like that here, too. I called and asked you, and you politely replied that the use of a vault was only for specific customers, which I took to mean: for cus-tomers who had a lot more than a couple hundred US dollars to protect. And then you asked, in all seriousness, why I couldn't just put the money and passports in a box and tie it tightly with some string?

For the first time in several weeks since moving to Korea, I laughed. I got off the phone and decided that one thing I would have to learn was simply to let go of my fears—and trust. Trust in what, I wasn't sure at the time. And I didn't put the money and passports in a box, tied up with string. I put it in a plastic bag and hid it behind the vanity mirror.

Ma'am, the Yogurt and Milk Seller

I am not sure which company you work for, but you wear a red and white striped bow tie with a mustard-colored uniform. It's not very becoming for the Asian skin tone, but in spite of that, you sell yogurt and milk with pride and a friendly smile. Your cooler is parked on the sidewalk in front of the bank near the elementary school. We became well acquainted — as well as two people who don't speak the same language could possibly be — because I used to teach at that elementary school, so I walked past you every day. Sometimes I ran into you at the bank because you would be taking a break, escaping the heat, monsoon rain or freezing wind.

I imagine that from your vantage point, day after day, you see all the children grow up, know who their best friends and mothers are. I bet you hear all the latest gossip from your regulars, the ones who stop to pick up a small carton of milk for coffee or cereal that day. If I could, I would have asked you what you think of the people in that neighborhood, what it's like to watch life happen on this street.

Waving hello to you each day as I walked to and from work

became a welcome routine, a sort of anchor in a time when everything felt new and unpredictable. You knew I couldn't speak Korean, so you would say a few things in English, like calling me *beauuutiful*, gesturing with your hand for emphasis. You often asked where my husband was and would say with the same dramatic voice and gesture, *haaandsome*. Indeed, all the 6th grade girls were in love with him. When I began to explore photography, you let me take a photo of you, even though you gestured that you felt old and unattractive.

Thank you for being a bright and smiling face, for making a new neighborhood and new life seem familiar.

Nurse, at Yeouido Park

You're probably not a nurse, and I don't actually know what you look like because when our paths crossed, I had my head buried in my husband's shoulder, ashamed. He was trying to teach me to ride a bike. After several attempts, I actually started riding—but I got scared when my husband let go, and I lost my balance, taking a huge spill. My shoulder was scraped and bleeding badly, but it was really my pride that was wounded. There I was, twenty-seven years old, still bike illiterate, surrounded by hundreds of little children confidently pedaling around me. I could feel their stares and wonder at the grown-up curled up on the ground crying.

We returned the rented bike, having only borrowed it for about 20 minutes. My husband asked if there was a first aid kit. I felt a cold spray sting my shoulder, a bandage gingerly applied, and my shirt pulled back into place. To my surprise, I heard my husband say "thank you for your help," in Korean, and that's when I realized it was a stranger who had bandaged my wound. I think you knew I'd be embarrassed, so by the time

I looked up, you had already turned and walked away. All I knew was that you were a young lady and that your act of kindness really touched me. Even though I had already been in Korea at least one year, I wasn't sure if I would ever learn to love it. I was having a hard time adjusting, but you gave me the strength to give Korea and Koreans another chance.

Hyunjin, Dabin and Heyum

I miss you three girls a lot. We lost touch a couple years ago, somewhere in between all the changes in your cell phone numbers. You both have probably completed your second year of high school by now. I often think of the little notes you would write to me. I didn't know any Korean at the time, so you all compiled a necessary list of vocabulary words and drew little pictures to illustrate the definitions. On my birthday, you all pooled your pocket money and bought me a little cell phone charm–a plastic teddy bear with my birth date printed on it. The charm hung on my phone long after the September 12 rubbed off. And then one day, it fell off somewhere in the city, and I felt sad.

I think of how you three would run up to me when I walked into class and say, "Hi, Teacher!" Hyunjin, you were the taller one and often raised your hand to answer questions during the lesson. Dabin, even though you were shy and didn't speak often, I knew the words were rattling around in your head—they just came out better on paper. Heyum, you weren't so great at English, but with your outgoing personality, you managed to find a way to tell me that you loved to dance and that your favorite color was purple. You all would listen intently as I taught, in spite of the fact that your other twenty-eight classmates were goofing off or completely disinterested. I didn't blame them. The curriculum was pretty boring, and the phrases I had to teach weren't very useful for meaningful conversation.

Maybe you could tell that I was really discouraged at your school. I felt like I couldn't make a difference in anyone's life because there were too many students and too few hours. It frustrated me that after six months, your classmates were still strangers to me. You see, I was really curious about what was going on in their heads. I wanted to know if they enjoyed school, if they had brothers or sisters, if their dads worked long hours and if they missed them. I wondered if they felt English was at all interesting, or just a necessary evil. I wished I could find out what they were saying to each other, and what made them laugh or cry, whether they preferred *tteokbokki* (spicy rice cakes) or ramen, if being a fifth grader was really hard and whether staying up till 1:00 am many nights of the week doing homework made them feel crazy.

Even after you all moved up to sixth grade and I wasn't your teacher anymore, I would receive text messages saying hi. I still didn't know much Korean at that point, and when I offered to take the three of you to a dog café in Hongdae, you had to call the café for me to get directions because I couldn't ask for them myself!

I hope you know that if you all hadn't done those sweet little things, like bringing me snacks on November 11, chocolate on Valentine's, or that Simpson's notebook for Teacher's Day, I really wouldn't have made it that year and a half I was at your school.

I think of you three often and wish you well. I hope your English is improving steadily and that you know that even if it's not perfect, it's not the end of the world. I know the pressure is mounting each year as you prepare to take college entrance exams and then move forward towards your careers. I know there will be a time when you begin to question your identity and self-worth — especially as young women — and the search for that answer can be a hard journey. I wish I could be there during that journey to let you each know how special you are. Thank you for the letters, presents and the inside jokes. You all for made my first few years as a teacher so memorable.

Korean Food

I confess, I have been snobbish towards you. I disdained you for your simple, straightforward flavors. The predictable ingredients bored me: garlic, onions, chili pepper and *kimchi*. I considered your acorn jelly, burnt rice crackers and meatless dishes to be beneath me. I kept looking amongst the varieties of side dishes for fresh vegetables, but all I found were pickled or salted ones. I couldn't understand why people loved ramen or why my students thought it was such a treat to eat barley hardtack. I don't know who did the English translation for the name of that snack, but it reminds me of something cowboys used to eat on long cattle drives across the United States several hundred years ago.

When we first moved to Korea, international food was much harder to find. I missed my Chinese food, cuisine made with a variety of spices resulting in a flavor that was mouth wateringly complex. I missed Lebanese *tabbouleh* and *kibbeh*. I missed quesadillas with real sour cream. I missed eating a huge salad with lots of toppings. I missed cupcakes with real buttercream frosting. I missed being able to cook a dish without worrying whether the ingredients were in season or not.

Korean Food, I turned a cold shoulder to you for so many reasons. But there you were, staring at me day after day in the traditional markets—huge wicker baskets of dried chili peppers, pots of homemade soybean paste and bouquets of garlic filling the back of a truck. There you were in the *bunsik* restaurants, menus with at least fifty different items—snacks, rice dishes, soups, noodles and dumplings.

Quietly, humbly, you waited for me to discover the true you and the people that are connected to your identity. And then I saw it. Your simplicity, your common ingredients were a reflection of war, famine and hard times in recent history. The pickled and salted dishes? They were made to survive inclement weather and economic instability. The acorn jelly and burnt rice snacks hint at your ability to make good of very little.

My taste in food and all the things I missed were an expression of the stability and wealth in my life in the United States. I used to view the ready availability of avocados from Mexico, kiwifruit from New Zealand, pre-made pesto from Italy and cheese from France with a sense of entitlement. I now understand that immediate access to fresh produce and ingredients from a variety of foreign countries is a luxury.

And so, Korean Food, I beg your pardon. We might not be best friends, but you've gained my respect. I've changed because of you. The rhythm of my life has been altered. Now I live and eat according to the seasons. I get excited when the summer rains end because I think of the persimmons that will soon arrive in the markets. I welcome the winter snow because it reminds me of when I first arrived in Korea, on February 28, 2009, just in time to catch the end of strawberry season. I've learned to cook many of your dishes from scratch and they are now staples in my weekly meal plan. Thanks to you, I've learned a few things about simplicity and resilience.

Korean Language Teacher

During the time that I studied Korean at the university, I had four different professors. They were all wonderful and I loved their classes. Like the others, you were always prepared, had very neat handwriting on the marker board and knew how to explain things simply and clearly. You were serious, though kind towards all of us. The only difference is that, among the four, you were the only one who was a wife and mother.

On the first day of class, you asked us to draw pictures on posters to introduce ourselves. I remember that in the middle of your poster, you drew a big pink heart, wrote *ddar* on it and told us you had a three-year-old daughter. I don't know why I felt this, but I sensed in your smile and tone of voice that you loved your little girl much more than you loved your husband — just a hunch.

In the middle of the term, we were practicing dialogues and learning to use the suffix "*-eulkkayo?*" to suggest an activity or invite someone to do something. I had to pretend that I was with a friend in my apartment, when suddenly the neighbor became very noisy. I had to ask my friend, "Shall we go somewhere else to talk?" You were going to pretend to be the noisy neighbor. In our textbook, the noisy neighbor was playing loud rap music.

But when you took on the role, you began a fake argument — one between a husband and wife. "Why did you come home so late? Where have you been? I hate you! Why are you so terrible?" you asked shrilly. You began to fake cry and slam doors. It could have been a scene out of a Korean drama, but something told me you weren't faking it, that you were too good at this role to pretend. It was a glimpse into your life. I didn't share these thoughts with any of my classmates.

A week after that, we were learning the grammatical structure for announcing resolutions or decisions, employing the suffix -*giro haesseoyo*. We took turns saying things like, "I will not eat junk food. I will go to bed early. I will exercise." When it was your turn to come up with a resolution, you said, "I will not drink beer before going to sleep at night." When we all stared, you nodded emphatically and said, "*Jinjja!*" ("Really!") And my heart sunk a little. At that point, I was sure things weren't well for you.

Towards the end of the term, I was sitting at my desk, looking over notes before you arrived for class when my friend whispered urgently, "Something is wrong with the teacher. I think she needs help passing out worksheets." I looked up and saw that your left eye was swollen and that you had some trouble walking. When my classmates jumped up to take the papers from your hand, you mumbled something about your ear hurting, perhaps to explain some difficulty with equilibrium.

Most people in the world are right-handed. It might be a long shot to say this, but I guessed that your husband punched you in the face with his right hand, resulting in your left eye getting wounded, and maybe your ear got hurt, too.

I wanted to cry, and ask, "*Seonsaengnim,* (Teacher), does anyone know about this? What's going on at home? Will you be okay?" But I didn't know the words in Korean and I wasn't sure if you would feel ashamed. I guessed that maybe, only we foreign students knew of your resolution to stop drinking before bedtime because we had no connection with your acquaintances or family members. If you wanted your troubles to remain hidden, we would be the last to publicize them. That day I told my friends with conviction that I was sure you were being abused. They didn't believe me. But I just knew.

Teacher, I want you to know that you don't have to be ashamed. Even though I can't understand what you're going through, I feel your pain by just seeing the sadness in your eyes. I wish my Korean wasn't so elementary so that I could have told you that it's okay to ask for help. I'm praying for you, your daughter, and your husband. Your husband must be very troubled and broken inside to treat you this way. Please don't give up hope. Maybe in time, with help, there can be healing for all three of you.

Mr. Nice Guard Man

Your job must be very boring—sitting in a tiny room all day, waiting for people to collect their packages, tell you their boiler is broken, asking you to call the repairman for help. Without an air conditioning unit, it gets so hot in the summer. There's a little radiator during winter, but I imagine it's still pretty chilly with the Siberian wind blowing in every time a resident swings the door open. You also look pretty old, too old for a job that shuts you in, sitting in a creaky office chair all night long. Your only company is the elderly man that sorts trash for recycling, two elderly women who clean the building, and the repairmen. You even have to be there on major holidays. I wonder if you'd rather be at home, lying on a warm floor or playing with your grandchildren. I am so glad you work at our *officetel*.[2] It's for all these reasons that I call you the Nice Guard Man, because I have yet to meet another guard man who was so nice. In fact, many that I've encountered are very rude.

---

[2] The word *officetel* is a Konglish (Korean + English) term to describe a studio that can be leased for business or residential purposes: office + hotel. See first footnote for more details about the term "Konglish."

Last year, one of the other guard men working in our building shouted at me for not understanding his question, banging on the mailboxes until I realized he was asking for my apartment number so he could retrieve my package. How was I supposed to know there were multiple ways to say the word for apartment number in Korean? All I heard was the word "lake," and I was sure he wasn't talking about a lake. I felt humiliated, knowing that he was comfortable treating me like that because I was female and younger than him.

But you're different, Mr. Nice Guard Man. In the three years that I have lived here, you have always been friendly and quick to say hello. Indeed, every resident who takes the time to greet you receives a huge smile. You say *aigo* to all of us younger residents like an old grandpa might, cooing upon seeing a cuddly infant face. When I was attending language school and dashing out of the elevator every morning to catch the 9:12 am train, you would send me off with the proper Korean greeting. When I returned in the afternoon, you were there to welcome me home.

Once, our boiler broke. I was afraid to go to the guardroom because you didn't have a consistent schedule and I didn't know who would be there. My Korean was so bad and I was afraid of being shouted at. So I came up with a plan: I would walk quickly past the guardroom to the mailboxes, and peek to see who was on duty. In case you weren't there, I could keep walking on by without attracting any attention from Mr. Mean Guard Man. What a relief to see you sitting in the chair, legs propped and your hat tilted over your eyes, napping. As soon as I knocked, you jumped up with a smile and watched me mime and stumble over words, promising to be upstairs as soon as possible with the repairman.

Last week, at 10:00 pm—when the baby was already asleep in her crib, and I was starting to nod off after a long day—the intercom phone inside our *officetel* started ringing—a loud and clear rendition of *Für Elise*, to be exact. My husband and I looked at each other in panic. He jumped up, slapped his hands over the speaker, in a vain attempt to muffle the ringing. I muttered curse words under my breath at whichever guard man was on duty that night, while simultaneously praying that the baby wouldn't wake up screaming. I am sure God was not amused by my hypocrisy. But maybe He'd forgive me for cursing, given the circumstances. We ignored the call and when it stopped ringing, my husband and finally let out a breath. The baby didn't wake.

Then, at 10:45 pm, it happened again. *Für Elise*, the muffling of the speaker, the cursing, holding our breath and then letting it out, very quietly. The baby whimpered, but didn't wake.

And then, at 11:15 pm, it happened *again*. This time, we didn't bother trying to muffle the speaker, we just stared at each other in the semi-darkness and I whisper-shouted to my husband, "You have to go down there and tell them to stop this!" Oh, the invasion of privacy and the complete lack of boundaries! I couldn't wait to leave this city! I was angry enough to go downstairs and scream at the guard man on duty in whatever Korean I knew. I was ready to wage war with the pent-up angst I had collected in the five years I had lived in Seoul.

A few minutes later my husband returned, creeping into the apartment, trying not to push our luck (does God believe in luck?) that our sweet baby—the best baby in the world—had not awakened. He was holding a huge box. It was a box of frozen, dried persimmons—the wildly expensive kind, specially wrapped for Lunar New Year. Apparently, it was you— Mr. Nice Guard Man—on duty. You were feeling urgent about the box of persimmons. You really wanted us to have them ASAP because they were expensive and must be stored in the freezer. You didn't want them to sit in the package room overnight to spoil.

And so, just because it was you—Mr. Nice Guard Man—I was pacified and laid down my verbal weapons. I thought of how endearing you were, to do something so ridiculous as to call us on the intercom phone late at night (well, late, according to our standards) because you wanted us to have persimmons. But you know what? We couldn't put them in the freezer because opening the freezer door and slamming it shut would have woken the baby. So we left them on the windowsill, confident that the wintery draft leaking in would keep them sufficiently chilled. In the morning, I checked the address label—it was meant for someone else who must have lived in our place in the past. My husband and I don't like dried persimmons. Not wanting them to go unappreciated, we gave them away to my husband's colleagues.

I will really miss you when we leave. I want to take a picture of you, but I don't want to embarrass you. I just want my daughter to know that in a city of thousands of guard men, you were the nicest one.

Mr. Manager at the Foreign Food Mart

I've shopped at your store for a very long time, since before the expansion, and before other foreign food stores opened around town. I still remember my first trip there. The aisles were so narrow that all the customers had to suck in their stomachs and press up against the shelves to let others by. That was one of the charms — that the customers actually let people by, saying "excuse me, pardon me." For a newly culture-shocked girl overwhelmed by the shoving typically found in the crowded Korean groceries, that was music to my ears. I took my time walking up and down the aisles, carefully filling my basket with black beans, cheese, spaghetti sauce, chickpeas, *chapati*, Nutella and Doritos — the latter being a special request from my husband. All the while, I was in awe because I heard you yell out for more produce in Korean to your local staff, ring up purchases in your native tongue and make light conversation with foreign customers in English. Wow! I envied your ease and fluency in all those languages.

I underestimated how much it would cost to buy all those

treasures that day. I was 2,700 *won* short so I told you to take the Doritos out (sorry, husband, but I couldn't sacrifice anything else, especially not the Nutella!) You waved it off with a smile, saying, "It's okay, next time you pay," and went ahead and included the Doritos in my shopping bag. And then I told you I forgot to get cilantro, so you should really take the Doritos out. You smiled again, handed me a bunch of cilantro and said, "No, free! You take it!" Free? I clutched my precious cilantro and became your customer for life.

Maybe it's common in your country to do business like that, but it certainly isn't common in mine. Something about your waving off 2,700 *won*, not even knowing if I'd be back in your store again, or that I'd even remember that I owed you money humbled me. It felt like home, like being amongst loving family, where little things are overlooked and quickly forgiven.

Each time I came, I'd endure a bus ride, two subway transfers and a hike up the hill to find your store. Then I'd endure public transport again, this time, hauling the weight of 50,000 *won* worth of groceries. After getting off at my neighborhood bus stop, I would hike up the mountain and four flights of stairs to the villa where my husband and I first lived. Once there, I'd unpack the bags that would satiate my culture-sickness, discovering little things you added when I wasn't looking—a can of Dr. Pepper, a pack of American gum, a piece of chocolate. As the years passed, I noticed that you began to give everyone a little extra something, even keeping an entire case of coconut juice behind the counter to pass out to everyone who bought a decent amount of items.

When Ramadan rolled around each year, you wore a *taquiya*

and exchanged special greetings with your Muslim customers. I wondered if it was hard to run a food store while fasting all day, but you continued to smile and act energetic. Once, I wished you a happy Ramadan and asked how your family was. You said that you didn't have a family. You didn't seem too worried, but I couldn't help but wonder if you missed your country and your people in Bangladesh.

About three years into my stay in Korea, a new foreign food store opened across the street. This shop wasn't as big as your newly expanded one, but it was brightly lit and very tidy. And the prices? They were surprisingly high, about thirty percent higher than yours. The owner was middle-aged, had green eyes and wore glasses. He didn't look very friendly, his eyes sort of following me around the store. I felt awkward about leaving without buying anything, so I grabbed a container of oatmeal — priced at 10,000 *won*. I asked if he'd be willing to discount, explaining that the store across the street, your store, sold it for 7,000 *won*. He scowled at me and said if it was cheaper over there, then I should just shop there! Yikes! I put the oatmeal down and left, sorry I had even dared to walk into your competitor's store.

By contrast, your kindness and generosity created a family-like atmosphere in your shop. When one of my articles was published in a local English-language newspaper, I showed it to you and your employees. While I perused the aisles looking for a treat to celebrate, I was proud to hear you read the article aloud, delighted that you all were laughing at the punch lines.

What a pleasure it has been, meeting you and coming to your store these past five years. We are moving soon, but when

I return to visit one day, I'll bring my daughter and introduce her to you — the person who sold me my first bag of Doritos and bunch of cilantro in Korea.

Miss Kimbap Roller at Jongno Kimbap
(near Eungam station, exit 4)

When my husband and I moved to Eungam-dong, we were overjoyed to find that right across the street from where we lived was a 24-hour Jongno Kimbap. Though it's a chain brand, it's tastier than the Kimbap Heavens typically found near subway stations in Seoul.

You worked there from ten o'clock in the morning until ten o'clock at night, seven days a week. You always had a smile, quickly looking over your shoulder to greet incoming customers while simultaneously making *kimbap*, rolling rice and vegetables into the seaweed wrapper in tidy rows. You sliced them cleanly, not like the nightshift *kimbap* roller. She always made hers in a loose and sloppy sort of way, so that the innards of each piece would dump out and I was left picking up the ingredients up individually, à la carte style. You also handled the register, and every so often went to check on the progress of the dumplings steaming out front. I imagine that your lower back must hurt from being on your feet all day; your shoulders and arms achy from long hours of rolling, slicing, packaging and lifting dumpling trays. But you never ceased to smile, to work efficiently and calmly without seeming stressed. One day, I'd like to be able to handle multiple tasks with that kind of resilience.

Once, I had to go there at seven o'clock in the morning because I had run out of rice and didn't have time to cook another pot. My husband's grandmother was staying over at our apartment and had just made *doenjang jjigae*, a stew. You see, I hadn't thought to cook rice in advance because she told me the night before that she typically ate bread and coffee for breakfast, which I thought was strange for an elderly Korean woman. She didn't eat rice or soup? I chalked it up to her time spent in Los Angeles and thought she'd probably changed her habits, so I planned to make a run to Paris Baguette the following morning for a fresh pastry and hot drink.

To my surprise, she woke before sunrise, turned on all the lights and began shouting as if I wasn't lying on the floor inches away from her, "Do you have *doenjjang*? Do you have vegetables?" She grabbed ingredients out of the fridge and noisily prepared her meal. In a daze, I remembered that I hadn't cooked any fresh rice, and it would take too long to have some ready by the time her stew was cooked.

I know that in Korean homes, you never have an empty rice cooker—there's always cooked rice waiting in the pot. But in Chinese homes, like the one in which I grew up, you make enough rice for one meal, empty out the cooker, clean it, and then leave it until it's time to prepare the next meal. I hadn't caught onto the practice of keeping a full pot of rice at the ready. But not to worry, I've since changed my ways.

So this is why I was at Jongno Kimbap that morning, hours before you would arrive, coming to get a single order of rice—a *gonggi bap*. I breezed in the door saying in Korean, "One *gonggi bap* to go please," like a pro. The two *ajummas*—middle-aged ladies—finishing their night shift were sitting at a table, probably exhausted, ready to return home. They stared at me as if I were an alien. "You can't get a single order of rice. You have to buy an entrée," they said. I stared back. "But all I need is a single order of rice." Hoping to elicit some sympathy, I explained that my grandmother had just made soup and we had run out of rice. It didn't work. Ajumma One said, "Well, go make some in the microwave."

"I don't have a microwave," I replied. Ajumma One gave Ajumma Two a look. And then they laughed. "Well, next time, you should prepare ahead," Ajumma Two said, in *ban mal*—a form of speech directed towards children, animals, and others considered inferior in status.

Hot tears of embarrassment and indignation filled my eyes, and I turned on my heel to make a hasty exit. Angry, and riceless, I returned to my apartment where my husband's grandmother contented herself with just stew and onion salad, no rice. I couldn't believe they wouldn't sell me a damn bowl of rice, and to top it off, to chastise me for asking! I knew that if you were there, you wouldn't have minded. You would have known that my husband and I were regulars. You would have taken pity on me, a foreigner who doesn't know to keep the rice pot full. After that, I never went there unless I knew you were on duty.

Over the course of three years, I came often to buy freshly steamed dumplings and *kimbap*. You saw me when I was pregnant and then again when my little girl was born, bundled in a fabric wrap, while I tried desperately to cover her with my down coat because at that time, I didn't have any of those expensive baby wearing carriers that moms really shouldn't live without in Korea. In those years, you never once looked at me strangely when I had odd requests, such as the time I finally decided to stop picking the yellow pickle out of the roll and asked you to just leave it out completely. I didn't know the word for yellow pickle, so I had to ask you to pronounce it slowly, three times. Another time, I asked you to make *kimbap* without egg while I was nursing because my baby was allergic to them. And then I left for the United States, staying seven months to get the support I needed as a new mother.

When I came back, I was relieved to find that you were still up front, rolling *kimbap*, calling out orders to the cook and checking the steaming trays of dumplings. You remembered me and commented to the cook in the back that the baby was all grown up.

It must be a sign that it's time for me to move on because a week ago, you stopped working there. And like so many other times in Seoul, the city of high turnovers, I didn't have a chance to say goodbye. So I'll say my goodbyes now by thanking you, and telling everyone I know about you. Thank you for doing your job with pride and a sense of contentment. In a world where people are racing to build their resumes and social networks to get ahead, you remind me that even being a *kimbap* roller, a very nice one, can make a difference in a person's life.

Mr. and Mrs. Taj Mahal

My husband and I discovered your restaurant on a very cold evening during our first winter in Seoul. It was beautifully decorated, clean and spacious. And, best of all, you both spoke English! We had recently moved from the United States where the economy had taken a dive in 2008, and we weren't used to spending the equivalent of forty-five dollars on two meals. But hey, we were new English teachers making the big bucks; we pushed away thoughts of economic troubles and happily dipped into our curries.

Your food did not disappoint. In fact, that week, we came back two more times for your forty-five dollar dinner! I don't know if you really cared (and why would you have?) but I had yet to build up a proper winter wardrobe. I was making do with a red hoodie, a short brown wool skirt, black fleece-lined tights, sand-colored sheepskin boots and a puffy white down coat. I was warm, but I felt ugly. And repetitive, because I wore it every time we were at your restaurant that week. Maybe my outfit helped you recognize my husband and me faster.

For the next several years, I ate at other Indian restaurants depending on where we were in the city. We ate in Gangnam, the Seoul Finance Center, Yeongdeongpo, Hongdae, Sinchon, and even one place all the way out in Bucheon. None was ever of the quality or price you offered. I was sold for life. I raved about your restaurant to anyone who would listen, dragging people there to partake in the wonder of your curries and samosas. Once, I hosted a bridal shower there and you both helped me light candles and prepare my handmade place settings. I referred my husband's co-workers to you for a business dinner, and lunched there with a Korean student who is now a professional ballerina in Germany. She didn't eat much because ballerinas don't each much in general, but I hope you know that she loved the food.

Mr. Taj Mahal, I know your last name is actually Madan because it says so on your business card. Mrs. Taj Mahal, you told me your name, but I don't exactly know how to pronounce it and never saw it written. I feel embarrassed that I could never say it properly. It sounded like "Sritsana," but I'm not sure. You told me that you went home to Nepal once a year to see your family, and you mentioned you have an adult son there. I wonder, do you feel sad living in Korea away from your son? Is he married? Do you have grandchildren there? Is Mr. Taj Mahal good to you?

A year and a half ago, I stopped going to your restaurant because I was getting pretty tired in my last trimester of pregnancy. Then, the baby arrived in the middle of winter. It was snowy and the streets were slick with ice, so I didn't get out much. When my husband showed up with his co-workers and told you, Mrs. Taj Mahal, that I was at home with the baby, you boxed up a meal for me—free of charge. You sent your best wishes and hoped I would bring in the baby to see her once I was less tired. You couldn't have known, but I had become severely depressed, and your meal reminded me that there was light in my darkened world. The food was wonderful, as usual. But I noticed two things: the lassi was thin and watery and the cilantro sauce for the samosas was brownish. That made me worried. All the Indian restaurants I have been to, even the Zagat rated one, serve watery lassis and brown samosa sauce. But you never did. Your lassis were thick and yogurt-y, the way I imagined it should be in your country (if there are indeed lassis in Nepal). Your cilantro sauce was always bright green, as if it was freshly made within the last hour or so. Your restaurant had never been really busy, and I worried business was getting worse.

When the baby turned 8 weeks old, I was having panic attacks and was more depressed than ever. I went away to America to be with my family, not knowing I would be gone for seven months. When I came back, one of the things I had on my to-do list was to visit you. I wanted to introduce you to my little girl and give you a huge hug for the meal you sent me, for knowing what being a new mother is like. When my husband and I finally got around to getting downtown with the baby to see you, your restaurant had disappeared. We panicked. We planned our whole day around visiting you, even skipping breakfast so we would be extra hungry and able to eat your food with relish. My husband asked the owner of the business next door if you and Mr. Taj Mahal had moved to another location. He said no, you guys had gone out of business. I could have cried.

I hope you know that your kindness meant the world when I was struggling to find meaning. Because your restaurant survived for several years, it meant that I also had a point of stability in Seoul. In those five years, I moved house three times, changed jobs, and said goodbye to so many friends. Through it all, your lassis, curries and samosas with green cilantro sauce kept me happy and satiated during those difficult seasons. I wish you the best, and I hope with all my heart that you both are well and enjoying time with your loved ones in Nepal.[3]

---

[3] Right before leaving Korea in 2014, I happened to eat at another Nepalese-owned restaurant in Seoul. I asked the staff if they knew the owners of Taj Mahal and what happened to them. They told me that the couple had moved back to Nepal just a few months back. As I prepared this piece for publishing, I searched the Internet, typing in variations of what I thought Mrs. Taj Mahal's name could be. After many attempts, I have come to the conclusion that her name was probably "Sirjana," the Nepalese word for creation.

Farewell 401, 1307 and 811

On February 28, 2014, I strapped my one-year old onto my torso in the baby carrier, grabbed my suitcase and hoisted a large bag onto my shoulder. I stared at the emptied *officetel*, memorizing its odd décor.

The previous owners had installed a chandelier with wiring encased in different colors of felt: blue, red, yellow, orange and green. On the back wall was a large pink wooden cutout, an artistic rendition of a tree. Branches bare, its cutout leaves were scattered strategically on the wall to create a windblown look. Some of the leaves ended up on the opposite wall or perched on the banister in the loft. In the corner where the pink tree was glued, my husband and I rigged light-blocking curtains to create a little nook, a makeshift nursery. Into that nook, we placed a crib and squeezed in a lime-green sofa that we rescued from the garbage collection area one night.

How does one say goodbye? Goodbye to the space where we first navigated the rocky road of parenthood. How does one say goodbye to five years of life in Korea—a considerable length of time for someone who has only been an adult for a little over a decade. I wasn't sure that day. Quietly, into the stillness, I said to the *officetel*, "We've had some hard times here, you and me. But we made it." I snapped a few photos on my camera, images that would later be lost, as the back was mistakenly opened, exposing the film inside.

I had wanted to cry for weeks, but had been too busy saying goodbye to friends, closing bank accounts, paying utility bills, packing, last-minute hospital visits and general mothering to have the privacy and space to do so. I found in that moment that I still couldn't bring myself to cry. There were still more things to do, and it was time to move on. I squared my shoulders, wheeled my luggage out the door to catch a cab to Gimpo, where my husband had already taken our other belongings to a friend's home. We would stay there for a few days before eventually departing the country.

Since my husband and I arrived in Seoul in 2009, we had lived in three places: one villa in a neighborhood called Gugi-dong, and two *officetels* in the same building in Eungam-dong.

Prior to relocating to Korea, we had been warned that our housing situation as English teachers would likely be much smaller than what we were accustomed to back home. To our surprise, we'd been placed in a twenty *pyeong* villa (about 900 square feet), a far cry from the seven *pyeong officetels* (about 250 square feet) our single colleagues were given.[4]

Our villa—Number 401 in Gugi-dong—was located at the top of a steep hill and four flights of stairs. We became accustomed to, but never excited to drag our groceries and liters of

---

[4] Contrary to images typically conjured by the word "villa," a *Korean* villa is not similar to an Italian getaway. Unlike the many thirty story apartment buildings in Seoul, a Korean villa is in a building no more than four stories high and has anywhere from one to three bedrooms. It is smaller, but similar in layout to an American apartment. *Pyeong* is a unit of measurement, unique to Korea.

drinking water all the way up—until one day, we discovered the word *baedal*: delivery. If we spent 30,000 *won* or more at the mini grocery store down the hill our purchases could be delivered for free! From that point on, we were relieved of our chore, but would feel guilty watching a middle-aged man trudge up the hill and stairs with forty-five liters of drinking water (essentially, 30,000 *won*'s worth) to our home with no tip, since tipping is not customary in Korea.

Making the most of our time in that spacious villa, we played badminton in the living room, albeit with caution, as our ceiling wasn't tall enough in some places to stand up. During our two Christmas parties there, we reminded our especially tall friends to watch their heads as they poured drinks in the corner, or entered the bathroom located on the other end of the sloped roof. For us, our morning routine in that space was approached with care. We would gingerly step onto the cold tile and take showers either kneeling or squatting on the floor.

In spite of its odd design, Number 401 was special because it had ample space to invite people over. A new English-teacher friend came with homemade ricotta cheese to stuff into ravioli. While we rolled out the dough, she shared about her perspective as a Korean adoptee. A Czech friend came to eat pizza that I made from scratch and "baked" in a frying pan—because, like the majority of Korean kitchens, ours didn't have an oven. She talked about the challenges of dating her Korean boyfriend— the kinds of cultural and linguistic difficulties that are often paired with international love. My husband met an Italian break dancer and invited him to cook a seafood dish and introduce us to his new Spanish roommate. When a friend struggled through a breakup one winter, we cooked Lebanese food, eating it while sitting on the heated floor, talking about the meaning of life.

After two years, I began looking for a new job, which meant our housing for two teachers contracted at the same school had to be given up.

And so we began a new, more economical and space-efficient life. Number 1307 was a seven *pyeong*, one-room *officetel* in Eungam-dong—a neighborhood in a prime location. We were right across from a subway stop and a stream leading to the Han River. The *officetel* was a plain space with a vaulted first-floor ceiling and a loft tucked in overhead. To get around the loft, we had to crawl. We couldn't fit a queen-sized mattress, so we bought two twin mattresses and set them perpendicular to each other instead of parallel. Trying to fall asleep on our first night, I experienced tightness in my chest, an unfamiliar feeling of claustrophobia. Night after night, our neighbors would stomp above my head. I called them The Elephants, making up stories about them playing Nintendo Wii in the dark.

Downstairs was different. With its vaulted ceiling, my husband and I were overjoyed—we could finally stand up! He walked about the first floor with his back straight and head held high. Ironically, what we had gained in height, we lost in width, particularly in the bathroom. We learned to shower with our arms near our sides and to shuffle around in a circle as we reached for soap or shampoo.

I decided that being in Number 1307 was a lesson in learning to live simply. In time, The Elephants moved out and the claustrophobia faded away. I became a pro at cooking in the tiny kitchen, chopping vegetables and meat on a microscopic-sized cutting board and discovering one-pot recipes to suit our lifestyle. I learned how to avoid bumping my right elbow into the side of the fridge or my left elbow into the wall by the stove. I trained myself to look up more slowly so that I wouldn't knock my head into the shelf right above the sink.

In the time that I was looking for work, Number 1307 served me well. It was where I punched out my first piece of writing for public consumption and became brave enough to write ten more articles for an online magazine in the two years my husband and I lived there. I walked joyfully to Emart multiple times a week, sometimes going twice in a day if I needed to buy rice. The first trip was to get all the groceries I could carry in my backpack. The second was to carry the rice. It was so refreshing to walk on flat pavement and ride an elevator to our floor. No more trudging up snowy hills in the winter or flights of stairs! I discovered the pleasure of being able to run all my errands in a half-mile radius. Compared to living near the mountains in Gugi-dong where commuting to and shopping at the supermarket was a half-day affair, it was a dream to go to the pharmacy, Emart, produce stand and butcher's shop on foot. Living in such a small space forced me to go out, much like the other residents in that neighborhood. Mothers frequently gathered by the stream to chat while their children played. At night, the barbeque restaurants lining the water were crowded with patrons chattering over the lively sizzle of meat and clinking of glasses.

But there's something about living in a space that consists only of a kitchen, a desk and bed. I couldn't put my finger on it for a long time. All I knew is that I often felt tired in the little studio. Much later I would realize what it was: there was no place to relax. The space was set up only for sleeping, cooking and working on the computer. There was no place to simply be. It was solely functional. What a luxury it is in America to have a room dedicated just for lounging! I was so used to having psychological space in my home to relax and to be able to invite others to do the same.

Following the birth of our daughter, Ji eun, it became clear that seven *pyeong* was no longer enough to meet our needs. After six weeks of tripping over diapers and laundry and struggling to bathe her in the tiny kitchen sink, we decided to move. Blessedly, Number 811, a twelve-*pyeong* one-room unit in the same building became available. With the help of one particular friend, we were able to put down the money for the deposit, while other friends borrowed shopping carts from Emart and tossed our belongings in them. Riding up and down the elevators, they shuffled between units until all of it had been piled in a heap in Number 811.

Amidst a stupor induced by sleepless nights as parents of an infant, we finally admitted that for us, living in Korea was no longer a sustainable lifestyle. I had been unable to find suitable work due to visa issues and living off of one income wouldn't help us build a future. In addition, watching Ji eun suffer from severe food allergy reactions weighed on me because I felt helpless. Although I could speak Korean passably, I was not fluent, and I lacked the necessary local know-how for seeking medical resources to treat her condition. Not having a community of friends or family who lived close by left us with the sense that we could never really feel rooted in Korea. The low-grade depression I had been coping with since my arrival in this country became full-blown after Ji eun's birth. Previously, I had been able to get by despite an underlying feeling of loneliness; I had come to accept it as part of living overseas. I don't believe it was an unusual experience—it's the sort of depression that typifies the life of a foreigner who is only partially able to speak the local language, and whose closest friends are transient expats. But motherhood is a different kind of life, one that demands consistent, stable community—especially one with fellow mothers in close proximity—to survive the major adjustments that come with learning to give your entire being to care for another.

As a short-term solution, my husband and I prayed about finding hired help to lend a hand with housework and baby care so that I could get some relief. A week later, a young Christian woman recommended by a close friend entered our lives. She showered us with her wisdom and nurturing spirit. Once, she volunteered to sit in our house at night—free of charge—in the dark, for three hours while Ji eun slept so that my husband and I could go see a movie. During the day as she was organizing our laundry and clutter, she found feathers—signs of angelic visitation, she said. More than a house helper, she became a very special friend. Even after my physical health completely broke down, she encouraged me to trust that God would see me through this difficult chapter of life. It was a humbling time, a time of great need and no place to hide it. That's the tricky thing about living in one room. No matter how large that room is, you have to face those needs. You never have a door to shut out the problems, never have a hallway to step into for a moment of respite, unless you decide to walk out the front door and give up on the idea of solving them all.

But we didn't give up, my husband, my daughter, my faithful friends and I. We pushed through the next few months until February 28, the final day of my husband's teaching contract and our lease. Ji eun sat in her play yard munching *ppong gwaja*, watching a children's show on the laptop while my husband and a Korean friend put all our suitcases and excess furniture on a hired truck. Leaving first, they transported the items to another friend's home where we would stay for a few days before departing the country. Meanwhile, I remained in the *officetel* with Ji eun for another few hours to do some last minute tidying up and sign documents for reclaiming our initial deposit.

And that is, I suppose, how you say goodbye to your home and a life abroad. You clean, you pack, you invite friends to remember the moments you shared, and then you close the door behind you, stepping into a new paradigm, a hopeful future.

Florida, United States, July 2016.

About the Author

Ruth M. Youn was born and raised in Texas and has had a life-long fascination with language and the lives of the people speaking them. Beginning with attending French classes at the age of eight, she has gone on to study university-level Spanish, Arabic and Korean. Ruth's travels have led her to France, Italy, Lebanon, South Korea, Taiwan, Malaysia, Bali, and the Philippines. Her passion is to tell real-life stories through the lens of empathy and compassion.

She lives in Florida with her photographer husband, Paul, and daughter, Ji eun.

Made in the USA
Columbia, SC
18 May 2020